HARRY'S HOMILIES

PRESCRIPTIONS

FOR

A BETTER

LIFE

BY

Harry L.S. Knopf, M.D.

1stBooks – rev. 8/6/01

INTRODUCTION

For the past 25 years, I have practiced medicine as an ophthalmologist. I have treated babies, children, young adults, mature adults, and elderly individuals. These wonderful patients have allowed me to become part of their lives, and I am grateful for their trust. Indeed, it is these encounters that have brought about many of these philosophical kernels of truth, which I have dubbed: Harry's Homilies.

In attempts to explain a problem or an outcome of surgery, I have resorted to terse statements that express the idea in as few words as possible. These aphorisms have come to me even as I conversed with patients. Sometimes as I talked, I pardoned myself for a moment to write the idea on a pad. The paragraphs that follow each aphorism came much later, as I huddled with the computer in the late night hours.

In 1994, the local medical journal (*St. Louis Metropolitan Medicine*) gave me the opportunity to publish my homilies. I am grateful to the journal's staff and my medical colleagues for encouragement to collect these into a book. Although many of the thoughts are directly applicable to medical care and addressed to my medical colleagues, I hope they will stir all readers to think anew about the various subjects I have covered. Perhaps one of these pages will change one person, help solve one problem, or bring on a smile. If that happens, the project definitely will have been worth it!

Preface

It is hard to believe I've "witnessed" Harry Knopf for most of my life — the result of initially bonding in medical school anatomy lab and having the good fortune to reflect on our careers nearly 40 years later.

Weathered skin, minor paunch and receding hairline aside, Harry hasn't changed a bit. He's remained the consummate optimist and foil for our anxieties. Not because he failed to recognize the gravity of our more vexing moments, but precisely because he saw through them to the larger opportunities beyond. He regularly made the difficult easy and the impossible irrelevant.

Harry is entirely without guile. My new bride sat expectantly as the guests of our first dinner party dove into her prized dessert. At about the time they were asking for seconds, Harry decided he loved it and enumerated what he suspected (correctly) were its contents. At his proud declaration, "raw eggs," all spoons sank to the table. My wife will never forgive or forget.

I'm delighted Harry has been persuaded to share his collected insights with a larger audience.

Alfred Sommer, M.D., M.H.S.
Dean, Johns Hopkins School of Public Health
Baltimore, Maryland

Preface

Harry Knopf, an esteemed practioner and teacher of the art and science of ophthalmology for over 25 years, has compiled his wise and timeless thoughts about life and relationships. These are inevitably complicated, busy, and fast-paced times, beset with mounting demands and burgeoning technology, in which it is increasingly difficult to control our lives — to apportion time for reflection, understanding, and giving of ourselves to our significant others and, as physicians, to our patients. Harry shares with us his good thoughts, both weighty and light, serious and humorous — but all pertinent to today's complex and hectic life styles. Pay attention; this is good and insightful reading.

William A. Peck, M.D.
Executive Vice-Chancellor for Medical Affairs and Dean
Washington University in Saint Louis
School of Medicine

Preface

Harry Knopf has been a faculty member of the Department of Ophthalmology and Visual Sciences at Washington University in St. Louis for more than 25 years. He has justifiably earned the reputation of an excellent physician, surgeon, and teacher. Dr. Knopf is a gregarious individual who radiates energy and a sense of optimism. He believes in people and the positive effect that people can have on one another. In this set of homilies, Dr. Knopf shares his warmth, humor, and vision of medicine as a healing art. His advice about caring for patients, assuming responsibility for our actions, and recognizing our fallibility can make us all better physicians.

Michael A. Kass, M.D.
Professor and Chairman
Department of Ophthalmology and Visual Sciences
Washington University in St. Louis
School of Medicine

DEDICATION and ACKNOWLEDGEMENTS

This book is dedicated to my wife, Karen, who so often was my muse.

I also acknowledge gratefully the help of my daughter, Joelyn, and my son, Aaron, for editing my sometimes-distorted syntax. (All those dollars invested in education were not wasted.) My daughter-in-law, Jennifer, and my son-in-law, Edward, always encouraged me. Grand-daughter, Evyn, made me smile. And my sister Ellen acted as agent and promoter.

Finally, I wish to thank Doris Wild Helmering, friend, patient, and author for her invaluable ideas about form and content.

Cover photo: Missouri Botanical Garden, St. Louis (provided by *PFtoknoPF*)

PART ONE

Patients and Patience

Being a physician is a privilege. Any physician who does not feel this way ought to re-examine his or her reasons for becoming a doctor. Yes, it satisfies the scientific curiosity to a great degree, but it reaches the peak of satisfaction in the area of human interaction. What could be more rewarding than providing comfort or cure to another person? I have often claimed that doctors and clergy are much the same: the former curing sick bodies, the latter soothing sick souls.

In this section of the book, I deal with the situations I have faced when talking with patients. Although I have addressed most of the rhetoric to my colleagues, I think that anyone who has been a patient will glean information about the kinds of things that cause consternation in the doctor-patient relationship. Without patients, there would be no real joy in learning and practicing medicine. It would merely be an academic exercise. Without patience, there would be no joy in any endeavor that involves two human beings.

Harry L.S. Knopf, M.D.

**The most important part of
caring for patients
is
CARING for patients.**

As a physician, I have been a matchmaker, confessor, entertainer, comforter, and healer. I have laughed and cried with the patients. I can still remember the sadness I felt when my first longtime patient in private practice died. I missed her. *Caring* is more than "taking care of." If you put yourself into a truly caring relationship, the rewards will be much greater than the effort.

Sometimes we can cure.
Oft'times we can comfort.
Always we can give compassion.

Practicing medicine is a dicey game. Caring for a sick person can be very rewarding or very frustrating. Our patients can be mean or loving. Likewise, we can be cold or compassionate. We physicians can become very defensive when we do not have a cure to offer. This may lead to a poor relationship with our patients. But always remember, our patients desire medical knowledge <u>and</u> compassion. More often you will be remembered for the latter and not the former.

Never deny a friend
a chance to be a friend.

Most physicians have met patients who complained that it was difficult for them to come to the office. They claim they don't like to bother their friends to bring them. I answer them that it is not a bother; it is privilege for friends to transport them to the appointment. What better gift can you give to a friend than allowing him or her to help you? That help is a friend's way of saying, "I love you." Don't deny them that.

Getting is good;
Giving is better.

Giving ignites that divine spark present in all of us. We physicians experience it each time we bring someone back to good health. The gratitude of our patients is as heartfelt as the care we gave, and it far exceeds any dollar value. The gift of giving thus creates two beneficiaries.

Relationships remain
after skills are exhausted.

Because my practice is more than 50 percent geriatric, I care for a number of patients with macular degeneration and other forms of blindness. This disease is particularly frustrating in that many of the functionally blind patients are otherwise healthy. It is important to them that I do not abandon them simply because I have no remedy for their vision loss. I see them on a regular basis and continue to test for other ocular abnormalities. They trust me to "care" for them. And I do. Our personal relationship transcends the disease and gives the patient that important sense of self-worth.

Even though the <u>disease</u> may be winning, don't give up on the person!

It may not be your fault,
but
it is always your responsibility.

My senior partner, now deceased, used to say: "If you don't want any complications, don't go to the operating room." Every time we perform surgery or give medical care to our patients, we physicians become their guardians and protectors. Like marriage vows, it is "for better or for worse." We would all *like* our results to be uniformly good, though we all know that they cannot be. Therefore, we must plan for the "train wrecks" and always "be there" for our patients. These days we worry about lawsuits for complications, but most folks never sue someone who worked hard to correct unforeseen complications. You don't sue a good friend.

You don't have to explain good.

When I see a patient during the post-operative recovery period for cataract surgery, I need do little explaining if the outcome has been favorable. Patients understand good results, because they can see well. On the other hand, those individuals with complications require counseling, explanation, encouragement, and patience — that is, your time. They do not understand the anatomy of the eye nor the reason there was a problem, but you need to help them grasp as much as they can. They need you to explain well, especially when it isn't good.

Optimism makes you try.
Wisdom makes you stop.

I keep this little saying on my wall to remind me of the way I think I should approach life. All of us have been guilty of attempting something that we knew, deep down, was not right for us. (I once thought I could fix the horn on my car. After I was towed to the dealer because the steering would not work, I was wiser.) Usually we learn from our encounter to stay away from such endeavors if they arise again.

This is most important in medical care. Wisdom comes through committing lots of mistakes during our endeavors. The skill gained by a wise person ensures that **each** mistake will **not** be repeated.

First the parents bring the children;
then the children bring the parents.

Some of us have had the experience of treating several generations in the same family. It is a wonderful privilege to be woven into the life-fabric of a family, to share in the triumphs and tragedies, the happiness and sadness that defines everyone's existence. It is difficult to witness the physical and mental deterioration of these patients. It is even more difficult if we ourselves are the children who bring our parents for treatment, and those deteriorating human beings are our own flesh and blood. Being a loving "adult child" or caring physician can be psychologically stressful, but somehow we doctor/children manage to muddle through, don't we??

Harry L.S. Knopf, M.D.

"Age" may be a "state of mind,"
but the aches and pains require little imagination.

I care for a great number of older people. Ophthalmic surgery concentrates on such problems as cataracts and glaucoma, diseases of the aged. Consequently, I hear lots of complaints about "arthur" itis and the accompanying discomfort it causes. Still, most of my "old folks" are good-natured about their problems. They accept the use of a cane or even a walker (with reluctance and resentment), and they keep trying to lead happy and productive lifes. Some of us who complain about far less would do well to take a lesson from some of these old soldiers.

Nature makes the rules,
I just work here.

As physicians, we are all too often faced with circumstances that are beyond our skills to alter. People become severely ill, and sometimes they die. In my specialty, blindness is most feared; and sometimes it is unavoidable. When we find these dire consequences of illness, we must not retreat but remain steadfast and strong: pillars of strength for our patients and their families. Even though we feel inadequate and even guilty about our inability to cure, we must not give in to this feeling. Although we do just "work here," we must accept all the responsibilities of the job, even when they are disappointing.

**Another man's problem
is easy to solve.
Another man's illness
is easy to endure.**

As physicians, we are the caretakers of the sick. We must remain detached to remain objective about decisions. Have you ever tried to take care of friends and family? The rules about that practice were promulgated for a reason — they are sound.

On the other hand, if we are too detached, we may be perceived of as aloof or uncaring. Letting our patients know that we understand without "feeling their pain" will go a long way in helping them recover. Truly, we can empathize without sympathy.

generosity begets generosity

We have all heard the phrase "what goes around, comes around." Most of us link it to misdeeds and negative actions. But it can work for good as well as evil. If you are kind and caring, your patients will respond in a similar way. If you make a mistake they will forgive — just as you forgive a parent, a sibling, or a child. If you are cold and unfeeling, they will act as you do. Then a mistake is a lawsuit! Also try the same attitude with your office staff. If you are generous with praise and fair with criticism, you will receive generosity in work and improved attitudes from them.

Try it — you'll like it!

**either
You get older
or
You don't!**

I have been an ophthalmologist for over 25 years. Much like a gerentologist, many of my patients are over the age of 65. Aging can be a traumatic affair for some patients, while others pass into old age and out of life with grace and charm. Although this little homily seems harsh, I think you will find that most seniors will take it good-naturedly.

Our bodily functions interact
like a row of dominoes:
Knock one down;
the entire line falls.

Patients often have a difficult time understanding the complex interactions of the various systems of our wonderfully integrated bodies. "How come my heart problem causes me to be short of breath?" "How come my anemia makes me short of breath, too?" "And why does bowel inflammation cause me to lose vision?" Too often we just brush off the question saying, "It's too complicated to explain." But most patients understand analogies, and they appreciate your attempts to keep them informed about their problems in language they can understand. So, the next time someone asks why can congestive heart failure gives them swollen feet and shortness of breath, reach in the toy drawer and get out those dominoes.

Self-confidence is merely
fear, thinly disguised.

Your patients expect it, your parents expect it, and what's more, *you* expect it: the ability to cure the sick. Unfortunately we physicians are victims of our own success. In bygone times, the expectations of the patients were lower; there was less pressure on us. Now we are expected to know - to heal - to cure. The stress is great, and we are ever so frail. One mistake and we demand (or the lawyers do) that we stop practicing medicine; we become flawed. We physicians turn to alcohol, drugs, or even suicide to assuage the guilt we feel. Well, I'm here to tell you that you are **not** infallible. You **will** make mistakes, and they will cost something — prestige, money, or even someone's health. But it is not the end of the world or your career. So repeat after me: "I am not perfect. I can never be perfect."

There now, doesn't that feel better?

If you have to advertise a virtue, chances are you don't have it.

K. Vuylsteke

A patient of mine, a lawyer, passed on this bit of sagacity during a conversation we were having about today's climate for our respective professions. Advertising itself is not evil. One must let the public know who you are and what you do. How well you do something or how much you know, however, is more easily judged by your results than your rhetoric. Patients soon learn if someone is sincere or "blowing smoke." In the meantime, a medical patient or legal client may be wooed by the promise of something, only to be disappointed by the failure of that promise: "Our surgery is perfect." "We always win our malpractice claims." Everything always succeeds; nothing ever fails.

Be careful what you promise; it may not be yours to deliver.

If you don't toot your own horn,
how will you join the orchestra?

No one likes a braggart. Such a blowhard irritates most of us. On the other hand, those who are shy about their abilities may be passed over for that job or position they desire. You must feel confident about your own abilities to practice medicine or to perform any other job. The important difference is that *others* will sing your praises while *you* toot the horn. Where's the happy medium? It's somewhere between the two; you just have to find it. Good luck!

good is relative
evil is absolute

There are definitely degrees of good: "good!" "very good!!" "not so good." There are no gradations for evil. It is absolute: absolutely bad — not kind o' or somewhat — just *bad*. Evil can creep up on you; it consumes you in small bites: a lie here, a cheat there. Upgrade the insurance code a little; pad the bill, just a little... Beware! You are on the proverbial slippery slope. You owe it to your patients, your family, and yourself to be good, not evil. As the Good Book says: "Happy is the man that hath not walked in the counsel of the wicked..." (Psalms 1:1)

Harry L.S. Knopf, M.D.

You don't know what you believe
until you find out it isn't true.

J.Ferry

A patient of mine passed on this saying to me, and I thought that it deserved a listen. How often do we defend dogma that we fully believe, only to find out that it is all false? Remember radiation of the thymus in the '50s? Or leeches for fever? Medical doctors have been guilty of passing on dogma for centuries. But now we have scientists who study *outcomes* and *trends* in an attempt to change our dogmatic beliefs. We can look to the near future to find out the best ways to cure and prevent diseases. Our computers will rescue us from doing the wrong thing, and we will be successful all the time! Sure, we're more sophisticated these days, better than those guys of yesteryear... aren't we?

There are many ways to be rich…
and poor.

It is an oft-observed fact that people of means may lead very sad lives while "poor folks" can be heard to express their great happiness with their meager lot. Look at our own situation: Physicians still enjoy good incomes, but practice may not be as much "fun" anymore. Physicians working in Third World countries for little or no compensation are satisfied by the good that they do. Who is richer, who the poorer? It depends on how _you_ measure HAPPINESS.

Harry L.S. Knopf, M.D.

KNOWLEDGE and EXPERIENCE
are the parents
of wisdom

We can learn by reading, it is true. But we do not become learned without a trial or test of some kind. We never remember anything half so well as the professor's question we missed at an oral exam. Experience, positive or negative, tempers the steel forged in that furnace of knowledge. This sword of wisdom can cut through the most difficult of problems and reveal the truth.

The enemy of *good* is better.

I have heard this quoted many times by surgical colleagues. How useful it is in the operating room or at the bedside. When something about therapy indicates that we are achieving a good result, our temptation is to try one more little thing to make it "perfect." Resist the urge, my friends. That last addition may be the beginning of an unending series of further complications. Perfection maybe the realization that "good" is enough.

**Lord,
make the words
I say today
sweet and tender.
For tomorrow,
I may have to eat them!**

Anonymous

I once saw this statement on a church announcement board. I have since heard it many times from others. How I wish I had practiced it! What we say and do today can turn back and bite us tomorrow. Always consider what you say carefully. As physicians we say things that patients remember for years. Try to ensure that what you say will sound good to you when you hear it said back.

•

I have drunk from wells
I did not dig;
Fires have warmed me
I did not build.

Anonymous

We physicians have been extremely lucky. Some may say that our luck is running out, but we still enjoy an income and a standard of living that is better than 95 percent of our patients. Give back — your time, your talent, your money. Help replenish those "wells" and stoke those "fires."

Harry L.S. Knopf, M.D.

Even crocks get cracks.

All of us physicians have had patients who perplex us with incessant calls and complaints. There's usually nothing wrong, and we come away from the encounter feeling angry and used. A professor of mine used to say: "Those who bother you the most need you the most." When I was an intern, we called these people "crocks." Now I think they are described in the more euphemistic term "worried well." Whatever we call them, it is our ethical duty to listen to and to assess their problems each time we hear from them. The day you dismiss them without a thought will be the day they are really sick.

So keep the glue handy. Often a cracked crock can be repaired to function good as new. And truth be told, wouldn't you miss those weekly calls?

A good doc dispenses care;
A great doc dispenses "caring."

All of us physicians have had the experience of being overburdened or overwhelmed by the stress of caring for sick people. But every once in a while, one of them makes you smile, and you know that all the effort is worth it. I have an octogenarian — soon to be "nona" — who writes me often. Last week she sent a letter that so tickled me that I asked her permission to share it with others. It contained some humorous passages about her experiences on a snowy road trip to her other doctor. The fact that she felt comfortable writing to me about her experience illustrates, I think, the rewards of an intimate relationship with your patients: sharing and understanding. Simply put, patients want to feel that **you, doctor,** really care about **them**.

It's a doc eat doc world out there.

My wife and I were discussing the current perils of managed care, when I said, "It sure has become a dog-eat-dog world out there." She responded, "You mean doc-eat-doc, don't you?" And she's correct. The managed-care wave has forced most specialists and some primary doctors to feed off the practices of other physicians: "I get the contract and you don't."

How sad it is that we physicians have been reduced to predatory animals. I can only hope that this phase of medicine will sink back into the netherworld from whence it came. Until then, do your best to respect your colleague. And, yes, do be your brother's keeper.

Loyalty is only dollar deep.

I remember growing up in the '50s how loyalty was a given for most people. You were loyal to your spouse, loyal to your company, loyal to your school, and loyal to your doctor. Today loyalty seems to be a trait found only in street gangs. Divorce plagues marriages; employers and employees know nothing about loyalty; and patients will flee from a doctor whom they have visited for years for less than a-dollar-a-day of difference in insurance premiums. We physicians should and must stay loyal to our patients and their well-being. Money or fickleness cannot drive us. As much as we may want to swear at the insurance companies and at some patients, we swore an oath before all this happened that supersedes any other.

Harry L.S. Knopf, M.D.

Keep your cottons till December.
Put your wool away in May.

In the Midwest, we are subject to what meteorologists call a Continental climate. We all know what this means: wide weather swings such as snow in the afternoon after shirtsleeves in the morning, tornadoes, whirling thunderstorms, etc. This analogy may also be applied to our "medical climate" of today. We physicians are buffeted about by the high winds and driving rain of managed care. We're never sure from day to day what the climate is going to be like. But if we have the right clothes in our medical closets and can survive the clouds and chill that currently surround us, then certainly *"the sun'll come out tomorrow; bet your bottom dollar that tomorrow there'll be sun!."*

**Sometimes, someone provides
so much *food for thought*
that it feels as though
I have overeaten.**

As a teacher, it is sometimes difficult to know how much to teach at one sitting. I often have a single day to teach medical students or residents all that I know about ophthalmic diseases. Trying to compress 25 years into 60 minutes is a daunting task. And try it after an on-call night when their eyes (and ears) are half-closed!

Teaching is not so different from doctor-patient interaction: knowing when to be quiet and when to talk; knowing when to say something funny or serious; understanding when silence will do.

Knowing when to stop.

Your patients will appreciate that.

Harry L.S. Knopf, M.D.

A doctor who is always *on* time,
may be one who has *no* time
for you!

I am chronically late for my patient appointments. I admit it. I am one of those physicians whom they complain about in the *Ladies' Home Journal,* because I make people wait. Well, I have a good excuse: People take time! I like to practice medicine that still gives me a one-on-one, face-to-face, you-me interaction. And talking takes time! I tell my patients that I will give them my time if they will give me theirs. Thus I am usually behind by an hour at the end of the day, because I did not budget as much time as patients thought they had purchased. (Better check my booking agency!) The end result of this shiftless, time-wasting attitude? Most of the time it is positive. Only a few patients have "walked" because of my tardiness. I always acknowledge that I value their time as well as mine. Apologies are usually accepted and understood... Keep some good reading material around!

A good reputation
is difficult to acquire
but easy to lose.

We all like to think of ourselves as esteemed. All of us want to be respected by our colleagues, our patients, our families, and our friends. After all, we are physicians: defenders of the underserved, guardians of the health of other human beings. We never speak slanderously of friends or colleagues. We are always honest in our dealings? Right? OK, sometimes we may adjust the diagnosis a little to help gain payment for our patients (and ourselves). OK, sometimes we whisper (or shout) things about others that were better left unsaid. Or don't you? Have you done anything to besmirch your reputation?

The Bible had it right: "A good name is better than precious oil" (Ecclesiastes 7:1). Remember that, and you will be remembered; forget that, and you will be forgotten.

Harry L.S. Knopf, M.D.

**It is better that people ask :
"Why did he (she) retire?"
than if they ask:
"Why didn't he retire?"**

We are all driven to maintain our reputations, our pride, and our skills. We don't like to admit that we are older, less competent, clumsy(?). Eventually, however, the edge one gains from having experience is overwhelmed by the difficulty one has in "keeping up." Whether by procrastination, fatigue, loss of interest, or other causes, most of us become a little jaded, modestly under-informed. When we recognize this, it is better to admit it and stop practicing. Develop a hobby, start a new career, "gas up" again. I would rather be remembered for the good physician I was than to become a poor physician and be pitied.

PART TWO

Life Lessons

Living is hard work. Some of us are born to wealth and a life of ease. Others are born into poverty and have to fight merely to exist. No matter what your birth status, however, there are no blueprints that can take you through life without difficulty. To use a sea analogy, there is no compass and no map. If we are lucky enough to learn about ourselves at a relatively young age, we can mature into adults who are confident and caring, as well as productive. On the other hand, there are some who are thrown about in the sea of life like a small boat in a storm. With good fortune, they make it to port in time to avoid a shipwreck.

The homilies in this section address many of the stresses and strains of living. Perhaps one of them will address a problem you have encountered and provide that "map" you need to get across the stormy sea.

Harry L.S. Knopf, M.D.

Life is like a fruitcake:
It is filled with all kinds
of fruits and nuts
and morsels
sweet and bitter.
Still, a slice of it is
pretty good.

There are good days and bad days, happy days and sad days. The important thing to remember is that there *are* days. Wake up with a smile — happy to be ready for another adventure: *TODAY*!

·

Harry L.S. Knopf, M.D.

It is better to die "young" than to live "old."

We all know people who are eternally young. Despite their chronological age, they are active, engaged, and vital individuals. They seemed to have dodged the ravages of aging — frailty of mind and body, senility, or Alzheimer's disease. We marvel at them, even as time eventually runs out and they die "young." And of course, we all know those individuals who live life as though they were already confined to a retirement home: fretful, dyspeptic, frail of mind and body through no fault of actual disease but more of psychological aging. We do our best to help them, but the task is daunting. Sometimes we are given a choice of how to live and how to die. What is yours?

The stream of life will flow right past
unless you jump in for a swim.

All of us grouse and moan at one time or another either that we are bored or that life has been unfair. If truth be told, however, our problems may be self-made. As Pogo once opined: "We have met the enemy and they is us." More often than not, our lives are shaped more by our own actions than by external forces. We can blame it on our genes, our wives, our kids, our jobs, etc. But if we look into the mirror and study the person looking back, we will see whose fault it really is. And now is the time to do something about it: Get up, get out, and go do it!

**In life,
the same lessons
are learned
over and over
again.**

We all would like to believe that we are smart enough to learn from our experiences: that certain things are to be sought after and other things avoided. In truth, however, many of us are "gamblers." "I know that if I try that again in a little different way, I can make it work this time!" Where is that little angel who sits on your shoulder (like we see in the cartoons) and says: "No, no, nooo"? What we <u>know</u> and what we <u>do</u> are often very different, and we must live the consequences of our actions. Remember this when it is time to pay the bill.

Don't try to understand life, just live it.

When some of us face adversity, we ask: "Why me? Did I do something to deserve this?!"

The answer is: "You probably didn't." It happens. No one can plan for it, and most people are not being "punished" for some misdeed. (I have often wondered why bad things don't happen to BAD people!) But, no matter what the reason, you'll have to face it anyway. Skip the questions, the remorse, and the whining. Almost everything is temporary, except death. So, deal with it, forget it, and go on living.

The only predictable in life
is
life's unpredictability.

Wouldn't it be great if every plan we made came out just the way we wanted? And every beginning had a predictable ending... BORING!!! Give me life's adventures any time! And don't give away the ending; I want to be there! In my diet, I like something more than meat and potatoes every day.

**Your show has a limited engagement.
Make your performance memorable**.

You only get one life. Events may help shape the course of that life, but we have ultimate control of its destination. Each day it is important to continually evaluate what we do. Make each day count for something. Do a good deed. Try a new restaurant. Walk home a different way. Meet someone new. Tell your spouse, your kids, your friends, and your parents that you love them. Life time is too precious to waste any of it.

Always keep your eye on the puck.
Always keep your stick on the ice.

Those of you who are hockey fans will recognize the metaphor: If you do not watch the puck, you'll lose track of the game. And "high-sticking" garners a penalty. Would that it were so simple in the game of life. But the rules still apply: Always keep your eye on your goals so you may work efficiently toward them. And never, never cheat to attain them. High-sticking in hockey or life will only result in injury to the victim and time in the penalty box for the perpetrator.

Life's only goal
should not be just the
acquisition of wealth.
Sometimes, more is less.

What do we hope to accomplish in our lives? A successful career? Extreme wealth? Celebrity status? I suppose so. But I think these are temporary goals. I was once asked what I thought my best accomplishment was. Without a hesitation, I said, "My family." And I still feel that way. Still, a pile of money AND my nice family would be OK.

Harry L.S. Knopf, M.D.

LIVING is simply
a series of adjustments.

It sounds trite to say that each day we must adjust to new situations. But sometimes the obvious escapes our notice. In an emergency room, things change almost minute to minute. The ER doctors are trained to anticipate these situations and to respond appropriately. Why then do some of us find it so difficult to treat our lives in the same way? We fret about things that could happen. We wail about things that did happen. And we talk incessantly about things that never happened! Why not take each day as it comes? Surely, we must as parents, spouses, breadwinners have some broad plan for our lives. But let us vow to be flexible and resilient. That way, good or bad, we can "take it in stride" and keep on walking.

Mountains and Valleys:
Best and Worst?

Language is a wonderful tool. We can use it to express our feelings and our thoughts. Sometimes we can even use the same words for two different meanings. Metaphors are the best way to demonstrate this. Take for example the word, *mountain.* One may use this word to express the very pinnacle of achievement. We speak about the person "climbing to the top." The top of a mountain is the top of the world. On the other hand, a *valley* often represents a low point in life. We speak about the "*valley* of despair," and the Bible describes those who walk through the "*valley* of the shadow of death."

But are these metaphors always accurate? We can also describe someone under a *mountain* of debt. And sometimes facing a crisis seems like climbing a *mountain.* The mountaintop is not glorious, only the very highest or worse part of the crisis. The winds swirl around, and the weather is awful. We can only hope that the other side of the mountain will bring about relief. And on the other side of the mountain is the *valley:* not the depths of despair, but the beautiful, green valley of hope. In this valley the air is warm, and the sun is shining.

I'd prefer to think of life as a series of mountains and valleys. Mountains represent those hardships that we must face and overcome. Climbing up and over these mountains is difficult, time-consuming, and often exhausting. But on the other side is that beautiful valley. We can see the mountain with its storms and daunting precipices. It does not move, but we can. We can walk in the valley and find a way to be happy and comfortable, distancing ourselves from the mountain until we face the next crisis. When we do, we can only hope that we have recovered from our previous trek over that last mountain. So let's get into our gear and begin the next climb.

With a blessing,
there is a burden.

A blessing may be defined differently by different people. When someone who is suffering finally succumbs, one may hear: "It was a *blessing*." A new baby also may be described similarly: a *blessing*. A blessing is, by most definitions, a favor from God. Thus, the dying and newborn may be a blessing in that God presumably has favored those whose prayers were heard. But it does not end there. We are blessed with the baby, but we must raise him or her to adulthood. Parents are often a blessing, but they may need much care in old age. The person who dies is presumably free of the burdens of life, but those who are left must carry on, saddened and depressed by the loss. Blessings carry a price, and it is our obligation to bear the burden, to return the favor to God.

Beware the hungry eye;
it consumes more than it surveys

Greed is NOT good, contrary to the statement by one of the characters in the motion picture "Wall Street" popular not so many years ago. Greed is consuming; it devours the greedy person as well as his quarry. In the end, one may acquire material things, but he or she will be left with nothingness. Weighed in the balance, things gained are not worth the loss of self.

Uncertainty is the rule.
The future is tomorrow morning.

Do you remember "the good old days"? You could count on your job, your wife, your family, and your friends. I can still hear Jimmy Stewart saying: "That's right, that's right." (Yes, it's the end of "It's A Wonderful Life" when he realizes that everything that was wrong can be righted through acts of kindness.) Right now, those days are NOT! You can't count on anything! We walk ahead, but it's a minefield of fears: Will I have a job tomorrow? Will my family be safe? Will my house be taken away? Wow! What a downer! But I am ever optimistic. If things change for the worse, they can change for the better, too. It can't get much tougher than this, can it? In a little while, things will improve! I believe it!!! "That's right, that's right."

Books are doors —
Computers, "windows."
Go in! Look out!

We are living in the "information age": the Internet, the World Wide Web, e-mail, voicemail. The computer is to information today what the printing press was to information in the Renaissance (or was it the Dark Ages?). But wait a minute! There is a difference. A book was and is a door to an imaginary world: an invitation to enter the writer's mind, imagination. It is interpretable individually, by each reader. It is solace and comfort. Is our computer all that? Perhaps, but it is also "right now" and "in your face." With computers there is little time to think, work it out, mull. E-mail says: "Do this YESTERDAY!" And there is no escape! *CLICK.* Close the WINDOWS. *CLICK.* SCREEN SAVER. Lie down, read, sleep, dream...

You can be born smart.
Wisdom you must acquire.

Have you ever heard the expression: "smart, but no common sense"? It applies to any number of people who are incredibly intelligent but cannot survive outside of a protected environment, because they do not know how to live! "Street smarts" is a kind of acquired wisdom that often serves one better than the "book smarts" of the more academic types. So savor your experiences, good and bad — remember them. They will serve to make you wise.

All sunshine and no rain:
a place where flowers never bloom.

We cannot understand good without evil, nor happiness without sadness.

Without darkness, what is light?
Without dullness, what is bright?

Life is full of opposites, and we must absorb the "bitter with the better" to become whole people. We never wish for hardships, but when they come, make the most of them to bounce back better than before.

Even if life is a
"bowl of cherries,"
you still have to spit out the pits!

I have often expressed my joy at being alive (sometimes to the dismay of those around me). For most of us, life is a joy. We have the pleasure of good jobs, good health, and loving families. I have been accused of being a Pollyanna, because there is so much in the world that is not like this view of life. But I think that if one weighs in the balance the good and bad of life, there are more sweet moments than sad ones — and definitely more cherry than pit!

**Words
can give eyes to the ears
and sight to the soul...
or they can destroy you.**

My wife and I had the opportunity to see a film called "The Postman." Filmed on a small island in Italy, it tells a story of how poetry changes the life of a poor, simple postman. The film is beautiful and touching, but the message of the power of words, especially poems, is compelling. We are all well aware of the saying: "The pen is mightier than the sword." Words can inflame or soothe, enliven the spirit or smother the soul. Even everyday encounters may have lasting consequences. The pen may not be a sword and the tongue not a dagger, but they can be razor sharp and cut both ways.

Only speak words that
will fit in your mouth.

Humility comes easily to some, while others chafe at the idea of behaving humbly. To the latter, humility connotes meekness and lack of "spine." But that definition stands at the end of several others in the dictionary. *Modesty* is the first, and this is the trait that best fits the idea of this homily. Modesty may seem to be weakness in some observers' eyes. But deeds speak louder than words: A modest person can show his worth without braggadocio. Let the person with empty boasts eat the "humble pie" when his deeds fail to measure up to his claims.

**Poke the fire.
Fan the flame.
There's still some heat
and light to come.**

<u>We</u> have entered a new millennium? Or have <u>we</u>? Some cultures — Chinese, Jewish — are thousands of years old. To them, two millennia are like two days. And there are Western cultures that predate the birth of Jesus (for which the millennium is an anniversary) by several centuries. Are the ideas from these times *passé*? Is new always better? I say, "No." Are you ready to give up because you are old? Phooey! What does age have to do with anything? The modern world may be 2,000 years old, the ancient world may be 10,000 or 20,000 years old, but who cares. It and we are here, and we go on.

Harry L.S. Knopf, M.D.

**For humans,
aging is less like wine
and more like bread.**

I have often marveled at the elderly people I see. They are so vibrant at 65, still active at 75, and for most, finally *old* at 85 and up. This is not to say that they are not "good" at that age, just "old." Like aging bread, aging humans get a bit dried out and maybe even a bit moldy. But some old bread makes excellent bread pudding! So even though those advancing years may not be "golden," they are still worth looking forward to.

Yesterday, I was someone else.
Today, I'll just be me.
Tomorrow is another day.
Who knows what I can be?

Never give up on yourself.

You have the resources and the skills to do anything and to be anything you want. Reality, of course, sometimes will obstruct your desired path. Even so, keeping a goal in sight will push you to do your best. And what if you fail? So what! Get up and try something else.

Never, ever give up on yourself.

Know who you are.
Be what you are.
Live as you are.

It is fashionable today to "get in touch" with your feelings. So much better to get in touch with your true self. Don't try to live someone else's dream of your life. Likewise, don't try to live someone else's lifestyle. If you will only look at what you have, it will look pretty good.

Days are like scrolls:
Write on them only what you want
remembered.

Bachya Ibn Pakuda, 11th Century

There is a biblical passage that states: A good reputation is worth more than precious oils. We are, all of us, defined and remembered by what we do in this world. Everyone remembers Willie Sutton or John Dillinger, historical figures. And we all know about Albert Schweitzer or Mother Theresa. Certainly these individuals are not written on the same pages, but written down they are in the history of the world. Your scroll is being written. What do you want it to say?

Harry L.S. Knopf, M.D.

It's not a crisis;
it's a metamorphosis!

For me, reaching the age of 50 brought on the proverbial midlife crisis. I was restless and disgruntled about the way things were going: pay cuts, paperwork, fatigue, aches and pains, blah, blah, blah. So what?! I was alive, functioning, and happy about most of my life: I had (and have) a great wife, two wonderful children, and an outstanding son-in-law and daughter-in-law. My brain still worked, and darn it, people liked me (I thought!). So this wasn't really a crisis as much as a *chrysalis*. And I was not a *caterpillar* but an *intermediate form* on the way to becoming a beautiful **butterfly** (with a limited lifespan, I know).

Life is a do-it-yourself kit.
Sorry, instructions not included.
Any complaints, please contact
THE MAKER.

We have all experienced times in our lives when we wished we had a book, a map, a guide... SOMETHING... *ANYTHING* that would get us through unscathed. When it was over, we were left with experience to help us with the next crisis. I guess this was how it was meant to be, and we're all stuck in the same boat. But some captains are better than others.

Life's gifts
are sometimes
poorly wrapped.

There are times when we feel overcome by adverse events: loss of money, loss of prestige, or, worst of all, loss of someone we love. It is hard to look inside and view these events as part of life and, perhaps, valuable to our growth as human beings. As steel is tempered by heat, we are strengthened by adversity. It is difficult to gain perspective, but you must. Do it. Use it. Move on.

Always look for that pony.
It's hard to hide something so obvious.

We all know the joke about the boy who was given a box of HORSE MANURE as a birthday present. When asked why he was so happy, he exclaimed:

"There's got to be a pony around here somewhere!"

That kind of optimism can get you through the toughest times. "Silver linings," ponies — anything that can take your mind off your troubles and send you toward a new and better place is worth a thought. Just keep looking, that pony has got to be around here someplace.

•

**Contentment
comes from the realization
of how much you already have.**

Almost every one of us would like to win the lottery. Wouldn't it be nice to have all the money that one ever could need? Maybe. But having great wealth has not always guaranteed great happiness. Wouldn't a better wish be that you would enjoy great health? Or even that you have a loving family? It isn't money that brings happiness, but love. There are certain things in life that aren't for sale.

Make a wish for

Almost any thing,

But not for every thing.

For if the latter is attained

And everything is gained,

Nothing will be left to

Make a wish for.

Harry L.S. Knopf, M.D.

PART THREE

Interpersonal Relations

How we behave toward other people may determine how happy we are in life. Friends, family, love enrich our existence and raise it above the humdrum of daily work. The lines from the popular Broadway show "Les Miserables" said it best: "To love another person is to see the face of God." Being greedy may make you rich in material goods but leaves you hollow inside. Loving another person fills you up and makes you whole.

The homilies that follow opine on how we deal with other people. Again, I am not sure that I have found the secret to a good marriage or a perfect friendship. But some of these nostrums tucked away in the back of your mind just might improve your next encounter with a fellow human being.
I hope so!

Harry L.S. Knopf, M.D.

Love
is like sweet wine:
it is to be enjoyed,
not analyzed.

I have good friends who like to demonstrate their powers at identifying a good wine. You know them: "This was a very good year for the White Chablis..." Now Manischewitz red rarely calls forth any superlatives, but it is sweet, and to some of us it is really good! So it is with love. It isn't seasonal or identifiable by vineyard or vintner. No sir! It's real Manischewitz love; it is simply sweet and always the same. Try some this season. Don't analyze why your love is so pleasurable, just drink up and enjoy!

Harry L.S. Knopf, M.D.

There's LOVE we do and
LOVE we say.

There're times LOVE's sad and
Times LOVE's gay.

But the thing 'bout LOVE that
Makes it OK is that

LOVE grows greater
When you give LOVE away.

A man is a boat,
Adrift on the sea of life.
Until he finds an anchor,
A person he calls wife.

On the premise that I will opine about anything, I am going to take on this subject — marriage. I love my wife. She is the other side of my face, my right hand, and my soul mate. I know that other husbands and wives have difficulties and that there are (too many) divorces. But when you find the right person, you wonder how you ever made it without her (or him). A good marriage is like a synergy of two antibiotics; neither one is as good individually as the combination of the two. And as a bonus, you often get rewards like children, and grandchildren, and great grandchildren, and... you understand.

It's a good thing, marriage. I approve! If you haven't tried it yet, try it! You'll love it!

If you want to hear a love song,
you have to go where the love is.

If you are sour and black of mood, you will rarely find yourself welcome in a crowd of happy people. For sure, the cockeyed optimist may get on your nerves. But I will take the latter before the former anytime. The music of laughter and happiness soothes the savage breast just as well as any notes from a horn... maybe even better.

Counting time is not so important as making time count.

Anonymous

My friend passed to me this little saying. And it points out one of the problems we have in today's busy world. We seem to have no time to do what we *want* to do, because we are so busy with things that we *must* do to survive. That is why it is so important to STOP! on occasion and look around you. Love your wife, hug your kids, and phone your folks. A few minutes of the proverbial "quality time" will make it seem that you've had a whole day off!

I would like to be known for my heart.
Not a lion's like Richard's,
Nor a hard one like Hannah's.
I would like to be known for my heart.

Perhaps soft or kind would describe,
But not quite right.
Too light, not right.
I would like to be known for my heart.

I'll be glad to be known for my heart.
When I am gone, I will know:
Both friend and foe will remark
that my heart was true.
I'll be glad to be known for that.

My heart
is happy and open and large.
My heart is full and loving.
I want to be remembered
for the love that it held.
I would love to be known for my heart.

Don't walk in front of me;
I may not follow.
Don't walk in back of me;
I may not lead.
Just walk beside me
and be my friend.

Anonymous

Friendships are sacred. True friends will understand when you don't want to talk or do something with them. They will "be there" when you need them and not intrude when you don't want intrusion. But friends can be hurt, and friendships can be broken. Don't abuse them.

Harry L.S. Knopf, M.D.

The root of
"RIGHTEOUS" is "RIGHT."

We are often asked to give to an organization because it is a charity. We give because of our "love" for those who are in need. We are charitable, loving. Beyond charity is righteousness: obeying a moral law that states it is our duty to do acts of love. Our fellow man deserves to be helped in time of trouble. So when you see the need for giving your time or your money or yourself, don't hesitate. Do the RIGHT thing!

All for one
and
All for one!

Whatever happened to sharing and generosity? There was a time (I think) when people shared with each other and helped one another. There was no thought of reward. Why have we drifted so far from these ideals? "What's in it for me?" is the first question we ask and the watchword of our society. Here's hoping that we regress and that "thanks!" is once more at the top of everyone's gratitude list.

**Praise can be given away
at no cost to the donor.
Praise received
has inestimable worth.**

I have been struck quite often by how a small amount of praise can bring about a large return of gratitude. This may be expressed directly or in indirect ways through hard work or favors. A "thank you" or "job well done" said when it has been done brings out the best in friends, employees, and, yes, even spouses. Your generosity with praise deserved is extremely important in these days of high stress and low pay. We could all use some... "Good job, and thanks a million!"

In most endeavors
success is just as likely as failure.

Sometimes you fail. But you cannot experience the sweet nectar of success without trying. Failure is a bitter fruit, but not poisonous. Remember what W. Somerset Maughm said: "Only a mediocre person is always at his best." Go for it!!

Harry L.S. Knopf, M.D.

Don't look back.
The view may be obstructed
by reality.

Memory is a funny thing. It can be good or bad, happy or sad, foggy or clear, long or short. Memory can be self-serving and selfish; memory can be altered. And then there is reality. If you want adjectives, try "naked," "glaring," "unblinking." Reality is, well, real! Unlike our memory, we cannot escape its fact. So the next time you think about something you've done, and each time the deed grows better and better, remember this: Reverie is not memory. And true memory is the backbone of reality. Sometimes you have to stiffen yours to _really_ remember.

Keep a list of memorable events:
Record all the good in
permanent ink.
Record all the bad in
pencil.
Better yet, record the bad with disappearing ink!

Life metes out many memorable occasions: births, deaths, marriages, divorces, illnesses, recoveries, triumphs, failures. Each makes its mark on our psyche, and each alters our subsequent behavior. Many of us dwell on the bad occasions, inscribing them indelibly in our memory books. They sour us on life and make our daily existence a burden. Wouldn't it be better to tear out those pages, leaving only the good memories? Next time something untoward occurs in your life, write it down for documentation, but use a pencil; this will make it much easier to erase later on.

Happiness is an amazing commodity:
share it, and you gain more happiness!

Sadness may likewise be shared,
but each who partakes is diminshed.

We all experience happy times and sad occurrences. Revel in the happiness and share it with friends. You will be all the better for the encounter. Friends may console you when you are sad, but it does no one a service to cause sadness in others because you have a misfortune. Misery does love company, but you gain only a *compagnie miserable.*

a recipe for happiness

½ cup tolerance
½ cup optimism
mix well

add one tablespoon self-assurance and
a pinch of self-doubt*

mix again with an equal part good luck

add sweet memories to your own taste and
a pinch of sadness**

mix again and serve immediately

> Note: make up fresh each day;
> unused leftovers tend to
> grow bitter very quickly.

* doubt adds spice to each decision
** a little sadness enhances sweet
   memories

I am *happy*,
because
I am

People have often asked me: "What makes you so happy?"

Well, today I finally arrived at an answer: "Because I am!"

I know that I am, I exist; I am I. Think about this: We feel — pain, pleasure, enjoyment, sadness. Animals certainly feel some of these physically, but do they know that they exist as individuals, distinct from their environment? Do you? Are you?

If happiness is due to the realization that I am, then the converse may be true: Sadness is brought on by the loss of yourself. Perhaps the problem with some of us is that we do not know who we are or even that we are. And that makes it a chore to just live life. Next time you feel something — anything — revel in the sensation. It tells you that you are here. And when the unique you and the unique me are gone, then you "are" no longer, and I "am" not.

"good enough" is often good enough
and sometimes better than "better"

Mediocrity is one of the biggest problems in our society. It is all-pervasive, affecting our education, our work standards, and our behavior. Everything seems to be "dumbed down." On the other hand, some of us are too preoccupied with perfection. "It has to be done right or not at all!" And this attitude may result in: "not at all!" There must be a happy medium between best and worst, and it is called *average*. What we need to strive for is raising the average so that "good enough" is truly good enough. Just remember to leave some room near the "top" for improvement, because once you arrive there, there is only one direction to go.

Harry L.S. Knopf, M.D.

Satisfaction supercedes salary?

It has always been important to me that I like what I am doing. Whether it is my profession, my hobby, or my social life, I desire satisfaction and enjoyment. But simply deriving satisfaction does not pay the bills! As professionals, each of us would like to be compensated for the work we do at a level commensurate with our education, responsibilities, and skills. So what happened? We can only hope that things will change before there are no professions with which we can be satisfied!

Aches and pains!
Tests and pills!
These are the price
of admission to
"old age."
The show is starting …

Ah, the "Golden Years." So many have described our dotage as a time of better days: happier, carefree. Would that it were so. Many of my patients describe their declining years as troublesome and painful: arthritis, heart trouble, and cancer. Not for sissies, to be sure.

But some of my seniors are just wonderful: active, upbeat, and vital. They are enjoying a golden age of lightened responsibility, more disposable income and a freer lifestyle. More power to them! I wish all of us to be so lucky.

For myself, I note only the first signs of aging: an ability to make decisions faster, 'cuz I've been there, done that!

Harry L.S. Knopf, M.D.

Medicine is the art of treating lots of diseases we cannot cure.

It is not a new concept to describe medicine as an art and a science. We have been schooled in this vein since our first year of training.

But how many of us have really thought about it? There are so many diseases that are chronic and even fatal. We "treat" these diseases knowing that they will never be "cured." The "art" of medicine is displayed by how well we treat the patient, despite the ravages of the disease. We cannot always cure, but we should always continue to treat to be constant to be THERE.

EPILOGUE

It has been said that words are cheap. I am here to tell you that this adage is only true on its face. In truth, words are hard to come by. Producing **these** words has been hard work! I hope that you, the reader, have derived some small measure of pleasure, insight, joy, enlightenment, or stimulation from the *Homilies.*

I would like to end with one more aphorism that sums up all of my philosophy about life and living:

LIFE IS AVAILABLE!
ACT NOW! THIS OFFER IS LIMITED,
AND IT WILL NOT BE REPEATED.

Carpe diem!

Printed in the United States
2041

9 780759 634305